you are beautiful

maybe i am too

Jocelyn Newport

First edition 2025

ISBN: 978-0-473-76688-7

Cover design by KVNO

jocenewport@gmail.com

For my children, Arabella, Daphne, and Harrison.

May poetry help you find the beauty in everything.

point of departure

near

far

transported

through time space

space from

where you were

finding where you are

is not

who you expected

nice to meet you here

new frontiers

sleepless

fearless

where it matters

her heart in a glass box now

always visible

and easily shattered

yet she carries it there

for her son

she will have many fears

and she will overcome them

she must

it's what a mother does

the beauty is she would

do that 10 million times over

living courageously for another

makes life all the more sweeter

wake with a plan

the day rises the sun is passing
he calls, he smiles, times slows, he's laughing
focused present treasures abound
eyes see clearly when time slows down

boxes to tick lists to cross
laundry to fold dishes to wash
a tiny grasp pull-pulls my hand
takes me to play in his imaginary land

time stretches again, i have all day
this is what matters all jobs can wait
what greater perfection could i achieve
if i dared allow this moment to leave

take the free fall

don't judge

don't think

surrender

be held

or let go

your connection to

magnificence

is a magnet

calling you home

imbalance

in balance

      is a holy grail

      a fairy wish

            on tip toes

            holding the line

            with no hands

hands are tied

      bound by the mind

      all that needs doing

            but life must be done

            where is the fun

                  hide and seek

                  on the balance beam

                        hard to know

                        what is a need

                        and what is a must

            it's hard to surrender

                  when trying to balance you know

Growing pains

This cold

is my reintegration

our bodies resist change

this cold

Its fight for stasis

I am change

I have a new story to tell

purging the old with sneezes

and many tissues

wading a swamp of congestion

unable to sleep to reintegrate

yet

but I will

I already have

in time my body will come round

and wonder

why it put up such a fight

as the aches fade from memory

and excitement sharpens my focus

once more

dissolution

things i previously held firm views on
have shifted
cloudy powder dissolved in water
leaving crystal clear nothing

things aren't always as they seem
my mind can change
and it should

attachment

want it

need it

can't live without it

easily transferred

to unhealthy obsession

non-attachment

waits

trusts

knows

the right things

already belong

love letter

it took 40 years

to know the true

value of my one

and only body

how fleeting this

time

contained within

daily i recite

love letters to

the only vessel

i know and

promise to take

care of it

affirmations

wishlists

i wonder what my

future self would say

would want

or not

she could say don't

dream or write a list

be where you are

allow yourself to

unfold

like the flower

you are

whose dreams

are you chasing anyway?

the doing dance

take a step
any direction
the waterfall
flows forward

do not build a dam
with indecision
unblock the way
with action

feedback loop

don't want

but need

to grow

not always

ready

or willing

to know

there's more work to do

late night shower followed by poetry

shower on

      clothes off

            do a wee (not in shower)

in shower

      soap on

            stand in steaming heat

shave legs

      brush teeth

            spin sway

face in spray

      water washing

            clean

revolution

circles round again
as i knew it would
incomplete revolution
a chance

fortune favours
courageous hearts and minds
mine is bruised
but brandished

a need to metamorphosize
into my own strength
vulnerability my weapon
protective shield

unarmed is the strongest way
to stand openhearted
trust the journey
the procession
         forward
                  marches on
         step into myself

poetry in motion

put kettle on

read article

open book

call a friend

read another article

answer text

feel tired

take a break

i really should work

not in the mood

answer another text

type a sentence

excuse myself

lots to unpack

for many days after a trip
thoughts remain
unpacked
in the bottom
of my mind

the joyful
are shared immediately
they were carry-on
for easy access

of the others
only the urgent
that need laundering
are dealt with
the rest
unwanted souvenirs
abandoned
like my bag
on the floor

letter to my daughters

my hope is that boredom is in your future
boredom will give your
mind a chance to wander stretch its legs
in wide open possibility

constant doing is tiring
endless consumption with
no room for contemplation is clipping your wings
i will not fill your day

i will gladly give you nothing
nothing to do nowhere to be
nothing to distract you
no one to conform to

nothing except your own perfect essence
and the chance to open your mind
by being
bored

curious

i wonder if it's ever
possible for you to know
just how much my world revolves around you
and in some ways
always will

all the things you teach me
things i never knew
i never knew
the person i aspire
to be
because of you
makes me hope
to live better in this world
all ways

i don't need you to know this
for me to experience
life as i do
because of you
is all the
thanks i need

i am only curious as to whether

it may cross your mind

one day

in the far distant future

when you find your priorities

not where you thought

they were

and you smile

to yourself

because it doesn't matter

you know you made

a beautiful thing

did all you could to

set the path

and let go

little ocean eyes

big energy tiny package

often aloof

it's a game

hide and seek

somewhere is a gem

pure bright love

generous spirit

who can't imagine unkindness

doesn't hide for long

only chooses when suits her

there's no telling

it's always on her terms

big deep blue sparkles

twinkling cheekiness

oh so astute

clever little one

in tune purposely out of step

with our drum

has her own that we cannot

even imagine

creative genius

loving imp

the magical now

see the world through the eyes of a poet

view from outside

the hue brightened

flickering images

sparkling enchantment

turn up the volume

real-life heightened

whispered secret undertones

crackle and hum

neverending banquet of hidden delights

beautiful consequence in forgotten moments

unnoticed by most

only enjoyed by tuning out

the regular rolling rhythm of

everyday life and tuning in

to the magical now

modern life

instead of checking
over our shoulders
for predators
we check our emails

notifications trigger
our reflexes
fight or flight
or swipe right

mates are found
through apps
instead of pheromones
attracted through mobile phones

our children learn
to push our buttons
so that we mute them
with digital distractions

we hardly notice
because we're not here

our brains uploaded

eyes glazed vacant stare

we rob ourselves

the satisfaction

of enjoying the real world

living in action

we compare reviews on temu

feeling we're busier

for some unnecessary item

that might make our lives easier

it's not meant to be easy

a million promises

i have so much
yet always want more
forever chasing the rush of new
if i only took time
rediscover what was before

knowing i don't need
false gods of delight
things won't buy us
more life
but they sparkle
so shiny so bright

blinkered eyes can't see
the cost of all this stuff
is me

swing between

quality time

connection

being there

sharing a laugh

a meal

a tear

a hug

a moment

needing to feel

relevant

status

valued

that there's something more

keep up with the jones's

how much of my life

should i spend

on making

my home

look nice

feel welcoming

25

like i have it all together

how much

should i spend

on friends who need

a shoulder

an ear

a mirror

or family who need support

my own wants and needs

it's all a transaction

one way

or another

money or time

experience or things

energy gained

or spent

why are we so preoccupied with

anything but

this moment?

drowning in things

you go about your day
i think about the curtains
that need cleaning

you take a break in the sun
i wonder when i'll recycle
the batteries i've collected

you enjoy your dinner
i browse the fridge to ensure
nothing goes to waste

you play with the children
i gather toys, laundry, dishes,
put them away for the millionth time

the world tells me
i don't have enough stuff
but i can't find an empty space

to rest my mind
while i flail about drowning in things

what am i looking for?

i open the app
expectant
hopeful
for what?

i have no idea
what i could
find that would
bring about
life-changing
joy
and yet i continue
to check
and check
       and check
a ceaseless itch

for what?

if i don't know
what i'm looking for
how can i find it?

15 minutes

just 15 minutes i said
a moment's respite
to see what's going on
in other worlds
to look into windows
unknown
to what end?

do i leave a trace
a like
a dopamine hit for someone else
or slink away into the shadows
of another
endless
scroll

disconnection deepens
thoughts and good
intentions framed and packaged
into neat little ideas
with no relation to the reality
behind any of us

do i know anyone better?
have i shown myself
to be a kind and thoughtful friend?
no
i have frittered
away 15 minutes
of my real life
just 15 minutes i said

15 minutes of progress
of contemplation
of joy
15 minutes that could
have given me momentum
confidence
gratitude
for this privileged life i lead

instead i was looking for meaning
where there is none
only the impression
that what i already have
is never going to live up to
this

unbeatable

algorithmic

mirage

everything

when i try to
do everything
be everything
to everyone
i find myself suddenly empty

high expectations
leave me low
too many ideals
best intentions
find myself falling short

time to exit stage left
rest reframe rewrite
a better script a better fit
with a role for everyone

so i don't need to
be everything

impact

if you wonder whether

you've made an impact

know that you've produced

an average of 114 kilograms

of plastic

each

year

of your

life

that will outlive you

by four to six

generations

existential thoughts

i

think

i might

be

having

an

existential

crisis

meno pause

truth sayers

no more

mrs nice lie

time to take back

space

step into my power

we live

inside

someone's dream

but i've

woken up

alone

and wondering

what's it all for?

why do we play along

estrogen-tinted glasses

today i believe myself

young

and vibrant

another day

i have all the failings

beauty industry warned of

tomorrow i may find

myself

anywhere between

depending

on my

estrogen levels

and ability to be kind

easy equals atrophy

when did we decide easy was the answer?
begin when you don't want to
start when you want to stop

easy is an illusion
a tool for beginners sure

but beyond it
lies a wasteland
of growth
       satisfaction
            enlightenment
                  and progress that means anything
just over there
       are the gains
that you keep missing
because you want easy

dad

what would you have done
with the world at your feet
are you happy now
have you lived the life you meant to lead

what are you proud of
what did you dream
do you feel like it's paid off
how you thought it would seem

you are my shoulders to stand on
you worked and you earned
to make us smart brave and strong
to give us the world

and when you're not here
i'll wonder if you knew
how i am who i am in part
because of you

forget me not

memories like
butterfly moments
paper thin, feather light

flutter and float
disappear as a
shadow in the sun

a sense remains
something
deeply known

lost connection
to the words
that describe

offline unplugged
untethered
no anchor

bobbing in endless
open oceans

eyes searching

empty horizons
for somewhere
to land

you are remembered
at the intersections
of lives you crossed

threads

thank you mother for being you
for teaching me to be me
the more you you are
the more i am free
to believe in me

thank you for life it is a gift
i can never repay
yet i hope in spending it well
you will be happy you gave it away

you paid it forward like your
mother and hers before
we each share the gift
unbroken thread gently unspooled

thank you for not telling me
how to use it what to make
allowing me to discover for
myself what paths to take

dual paths

always there
all ways there
omnipresent open arms
interwoven unspooled
entwined
she walks beside me

connected
together though not
all i do
an echo of her
shimmering through time

how can i make
a shadow proud
unseeing faceless
cannot hear
or feel
am aware always
of presence there
silent connection
duality

other people's hurts

we can't take them away
but sit with them in it
and be there

they need to find their own way through
it's not something for us
to bear

helplessness searching for something to grasp
is its own kind of
challenging delicate task

being a foundation standing most strong
so they can rebuild when
sadness has gone

a big undertaking at times but needs to be done
that's how you really
and truly
take care of
someone

my sister max

a wished-for gift
a sister for me
a real baby doll
a little girl's dream

8 years my junior
deep sisterly bond
made me laugh and cry
our friendship is strong

31 years since
she first made me brave
made me proud and gave me
reason to behave

still my friend
now an aunt as well
sunshine in my life
always there to help

words are not enough
thanks to accord

for her presence in my life

my lucky reward

stella and grace

stella misses drizzly days
at motorway service centres
grace sleeps
vision of angel
perfectly at peace

two pounamu fishhooks
two hearts ready for
brave new life

stella reads bedtime stories
on the plane
grace is spellbound
her mother-love radiates
crackles like a sparkler

magical mike

most magnificent muse

makes music ♪♪

(and money 💰)

many memorable moments

moving me

must make more

my magical mate

mike 💕

butterflies

chasing ideas all day
feels exciting
thrilling
enticing
i think when i get a chance
to catch them they'll be
surprising
delighting

except they're butterflies
hard to pin down
pretty
fleeting
up close they're mesmerizing
i don't know how to put them
together
meeting

glimmering dust where
they hovered so close
fading
haunting

they flutter out of reach

tomorrow i'll find them

glowing

taunting

again i'll be chasing

mirage vapours

reaching

lurching

for just one catch is worth the rest

all the wanting

hoping

searching

maybe i should get a net

resistance is futile

futile resistance is

is futile resistance

futile is resistance

(written while resisting writing)

last dance

creativity loves the last dance

when you've worn yourself out sore feet broken shoes

she likes it best at the end of a road

out of gas out of money directionless no map to peruse

entertained by excuses she may

throw you a bone to keep the dog from eating your homework

a defeat or disaster piques her interest

difficult times ahead make her presence more than a perk

a "no" tickles her fancy can't help not this time

locked doors barred windows no obvious way round

she's a fickle though generous lady who likes it best

you may have guessed when you have to try harder i have found

sensitive souls

the creative

house of cards

precarious

most exquisite view

out here

on the edge

long way down

fast free fall

longer way back up

more beauty

to be found

on the journey

poets are magicians

conjuring magic

from thin air

with only words

a sunset appears

bush walk

bath in tree air
connect to
everythingness

body walks
head clears
sunshine sprinkles
through canopy sieve

cicadas electrify
sizzling transmission
reaching tendrils
climbing claiming

for moments i forget
to be anything other
remembering where
i belong

forest whispers
collective consciousness
held in swaying boughs

daily bread

i need my bread
its measured magic
weighed and stirred
poured and baked

the oven heat
steadily radiant
transforms dough
a miraculous process

the steaming crust
its pillowy crumb
cooled and sliced
buttered and tasted

and then i'm fed
happily sated
simple joy
glad i waited

coffee

luscious molten black

daily ritual

extracted and poured

delightful sipped

bitter remedy for new day

cushions

oh comfortable square
oxymoron?

i spent a day
obsessing

imagining how my
life would change

with your colourful outlook
your generous plushness

you inspire me!

keepsakes

draw full of stuff

wherever i go

in case i need it

squirreling away maybes

for another day

that might never come

waste not want not

childhood mantra

what if i need it

then i have it

useful items pens

balms tissues tokens

moments captured

fairies in the wind

from dandelion clocks

trapped in drawer

museum time capsule

always adding to

neverending collection

moving place to place

in case

forgotten things

dropped tucked

hidden away

once exciting

full of promises

time has moved on

too many other

treasures to be found

and later

forgotten

tucked

hidden

      away

faded beauty

great

yarmouth was once

now a faded beauty

she razzle-dazzled

whirled in a crowd

wonderment

people flocked

until

they stopped

sea air stripped

and whipped

relentlessly

those who stayed

weathered and worn

bent into

ice breeze

some remain

a snow globe

time capsule

the heart still here

though the bones are bare

you can imagine

charming lady

irresistible belle of the ball

that was

highlands

misty hues

gradient fog

of green

shades of haze

granite rock

ledges edges

jutting outcrops

bare back of scottish highlands

bravely borne

against elements

forging northward

where only the

courageous go

friday

night yawns like a tennis match

one love 40 love game set

and the players proceed to bed

reset for the weekend instead

no matter how busy the day

friday nights always end this way

bed wars

whose turn she said

it's mine, i want to sleep in this bed

not fair she replied you had last night

you can have tomorrow's turn alright

i'm tired can we talk about it in morning

no it must be settled now, no stalling

you know you have your own beds

yes but we want to sleep in yours she said

not lice to share

when it's thrice in the year
you've experienced lice in the hair
you develop ptsd reactions of fear
of the lice you wouldn't like to share

sick

muffle-headed
fog sniff snort
snargle cough

snuffle-bedded
clog stiff short
bargle boff

ruffle-wedded
bog biff balk
wargle rough

cuffle-saided
slog diff dork
dargle nuff

i hope to
feel
better
soon

sick babe

hold space

see you through

the night

be there

hold on tight

wait for

your cherub face

smiling eyes

ode to mama of the sick

mama hang in there

ride the wave

you'll both get through

if you hold space

let all else go

be his all

and smiling eyes will

greet you again

most beautiful reward

sleep

warm sleep
covers me whole
holds me deep
soundly
heavy
soaked through

morning light cracks
eyes crease like
crumpled sheets
blink resist

inhale new day
body still warm
heavy with sleep
pillow-cradled mind
whirrs into present now

body follows
slowly stirs
hot tea helps

greetings

twittering chirrups

crisp air lifts

stirs my spirit

window ajar

inviting in the day

washing line

naked thread

vulnerable bare

waits

peg by peg adorned

fluttering feathers

tickling the air

priorities

i prioritised

making

tea

swimming

time slows

weightlessness

rhythmic motion

held breath

slow release

little kicks

fast and neat

lap again

reach the end

breath by breath

counting them

new lap

fresh start

powerful glide

pumping heart

up then down

few to go

nearly there

not too slow

carry on

lungs flushed

final push

legs are long

paddling strong

stroke stroke stroke glide

outstretched arms

meet the side

smile wide!

creative life

i have created life

i am

created life

how much more

creation needs

to be

leaves

give it up

why do you hold on to your ideas

why not let them fall away

like autumn leaves

new eyes

shedding old skin
i can see from outside
looking in
what is no longer needed

brave lightness
freedom of forgetting
all the ordered things
that were

where i was

beyond constellations

beyond constellations

shadows are nothing

when you shine

a star is born

About the Author

Jocelyn Newport is a creative living in Auckland with her composer husband and their three children. This collection of poetry was compiled to rediscover the joy of making art on her own terms.

Acknowledgments

Thank you to my family and friends who have always encouraged my creativity and championed me all the way.

Thank you to Mikee for being a first reader, editor and enabler of me regaining my creative authority.

Thank you to Dee for sharing poetry with me since birth and for testing the order and flow of this collection.

Thank you to Zog for covering me at the 11th hour.

Thank you to Arabella, Daphne and Harrison for being your magical selves and inspiring me to be my own best self.

Thank you Dear Reader, for taking the time to stop by. I hope that something in these pages resonates or brings you joy.

www.ingramcontent.com/pod-product-compliance
Lightning Source LLC
Chambersburg PA
CBHW031539040426
42445CB00010B/617